FOLLOW ME ON THIS

STACY DYSON

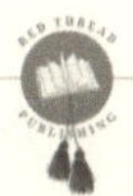

Red Thread Publishing LLC. 2021

Write to info@redthreadbooks.com if you are interested in publishing with Red Thread Publishing. Learn more about publications or foreign rights acquisitions of our catalogue of books: www.redthreadbooks.com

Ebook ISBN: 978-1-955683-02-9

Paperback ISBN: 978-1-955683-03-6

This book is for every person who shaped my first ten years in San Diego. I'm not even about to try and call every name; you know who you are. (And if you don't, then you are past praying for.) Y'all helped me keep my head up, held my hand, had my back, and let me hang onto what we laughingly refer to as my "sanity". It truly would be impossible for me to love you more.

But ESPECIALLY..

My sistergirl, Susana Bartolomeo...Honey, I swear I'm making it to Argentina for Christmas before neither of us is interested in whistling at surfer boys anymore. (So, yeah, we've got a minute).

Ms Rebecca Romani—I have the sneaking suspicion that you will be late to accept your Pulitzer. But I promise I will make them wait for you.

Mx Shane Parmely—one of the few people who understand when to leave me alone and when to get in my way. You haven't been wrong once, Sugar. Not once.

All the artists, venue orders, hot-shots poets, and audience members who let me "work it on out". My "voices and choices" breathe easier because of you.

My Colorado Crew—y'all kept the door open for me. Thank you. And last, but never least...

My Jamaican One—because every other heartbeat is still yours

Je t'aime, je t'adore —Stacy

CONTENTS

FOREWORD

I never seem to be working on the book I had planned. At this stage of my career, I had mapped out a sort of Greatest Hits thing... a book detailing a decade never even crossed my mind. But I started to think... always dangerous... and it occurred to me, in not the gentlest way and language, that the last 10 years of my life in this place defined me more than any other time of my life.

I have gone through an entire life cycle in this place—birth (new poetic voices), death (broken heart—a FEW times), and every single sigh or celebration in between. Some of it was HIGHLY unpleasant. A lot of it was beauty and joy incarnate; I have been very blessed and very lucky. And I think, I *know*, this is where I meant when I kept saying "I need someplace where I can breathe all the time."

The collection before this, LOVELY AND SUFFERING, was all about a year nobody was ready for. This collection explains the voices and people that gave me a fighting chance. The last collection is about how I made it through.

This one will show you what made me able to.

LYRIC I

PORTRAITS

1

BECKON

This is just a simple song

I tell you it quick and right as a summer rainfall

sweet and done through as a good cobbler or a preacher caught
sinnin'

this is Beckon's tale

and so many like her

maybe never should-a been

Beckon's mother was a Lovelace woman

soft scent, light foot, sweet voice

Lovelace women were known for two things

beauty and bowing to God

church-goin'/ hymn-proud /white-glove women

who gave no quarter and took no tea for the fever

SaintJohns—Beckon's daddy's people

ran wild

raised hell, whores, and gamblers

but their men could charm the wet from water

and their women could sing

jump-shout blues, wail and moan, jukebox jive, gospel

lay a note of music along-side one of them

and they would tease it, coax it, enslave it

then make it fly

and Beckon, with hair black like the sheen of a raven's throat

eye cinnabar gold, skin colored deep-honey

inherited her mother's beauty and her father's heart

her granmama Clare on her daddy side

soprano

and her granna Esther Sue on her mama side

firm belief

that anything she laid hand to was righteous

and needing to be correct

.   .   .

Beckon

baptized Rebecca Ruth

got her name from come runnin' when her mama called

or her daddy smiled

she knew better

see, Lovelace women had steel spines, heavy hands, and heard no excuses

Beckon knew she better jump when mama called her name

Beckon's daddy loved her

the best way

games in the clearing 'fore bed

stories when the rainstorm scared her

a stern face and light switchin' 'cross her legs

to keep her mama from doin' worse

sometimes, spirit her right out of Mama's chores to come swim

or visit kinfolk

or just sit idle

tastin' of the air and singing

"Courtin' sin", Mama said

Beckon's daddy say

"Don't you put no tether on my girl.

You let her run til she give out.

The world come bring hard times to her heart soon enough."

Beckon's daddy left her 12th year

coal-colored gal with a sweet face, some money

and a switch Beckon's granna on her mama side

said could sure 'nuff beat somebody to death

Beckon's daddy went runnin'

see

SaintJohn men were not famous for sticking by

if something looked better

now, I already said Beckon's mama was a pretty woman

a hard-working-God-believing-good

pretty woman

and this night-black gal weren't no prettier

but she weren't no good

and most men (especially a SaintJohn man)

faced with the choice

will choose no good

the dust he kicked up leavin' town

made Beckon's eyes tear for the rest of her life

any kiss or message he sent breezing by

got lost in the echo of the wind

that blew her cold and disconsolate

hard times came to Beckon sure 'nuff

and soon

see

folk called her name for a different reason now

in a different way

'cause Beckon went from pretty to make him-wanna-leave-home

almost overnight

a hard edge even at 13 turned tempered as a sword blade by 15

some 'cause of her daddy

but more at her mama's hands

her mama's hand at the end of a magnolia switch

locking the door to her room

flying across Beckon's face and landing on both cheeks

angry, often

her child would not be some hip-switchin' 'ho like her daddy had run

off with

hard prayers, hard words, hard hands

across her butt and backside

it made no difference to Beckon

she sneaked out/ ran away/ bore her mother's cross

silent

SaintJohn blood calling like wild birds will

fallin' across winter skies

"Sweet as anything", they said

"Fast li'l somethin' ", they said

Rebecca Ruth called Beckon

drew stares and envy and whispers

drew down her mama's wrath

and never minded, 'cause she knew

anything she laid her hand to was righteous

and Beckon set her mind on finding her daddy

her worth

in the menfolk passed her every way

still sang just as high and light in church

minded her mama when she took ill and died

wasted by hate and bitterness

hot and ugly as the sin Lovelace women

set their lives against

.   .   .

"She a good daughter", they said

"Triflin' slut, probably glad her mama gone, too" they said

Beckon paid no mind, her mission took her searching

eyes and hearts and bodies

eager to prove they could be what she needed

and men ...men made love to her because they had no choice

to deny themselves her beauty/ her walk/ her time

would be as if a woman denied the scent and sight of a

mystic rose

nothin' ugly or wrong in what they did or what she wanted

what they tried to provide

just sad, mostly

they never left angry

just down and confused

vowing that the next woman would not find them lacking

leave them wondering and wistful

Beckon cried most nights

feeling the sting of the dust her daddy kicked up leaving her

blow like Arabian sands

across her soul

·　·　·

Beckon prayed most nights

knees pooling blood red as fire-star

heart so heavy like to break an angel's spirit

or a blind man's faith in the blues

took lover after lover, never married

took lover after lover, never had children

took lover/ after heartache/ after tears/ after prayer

never stopped seeking her daddy

her worth

never found either one

Rebecca Ruth called Beckon

never stopped praying

she was a Lovelace woman all throughout

like her granna Esther Sue on her mama side

a SaintJohn woman, sure and stubborn like her daddy mama Clare

sang church songs and blues notes

prayed hard, ran wild

til most of the world's hard times nested in her hair

and hands

and hope

.   .   .

no man, no children

no daddy comin' back

no tether on her daddy's gal

connected to nothing but

soft scent/ sweet voice/ wild ways

(but never a wicked heart)

Beckon lasted long past sense

lived hard in memory

and left here

on a wind like her daddy never sent a message back on

soul pockmarked with bitter and disappointment

like what had killed her mama

put her wanna-be 'longside a single dream

coaxed it, laid enslaved by it

and made herself

fly away.

2

———

FOR MARGARET

The lacework in her memory

Je Reviens at wrist and the hollow of her throat

a song that caught moonlight in her hair

for him

she's worn it since before

a drop is enough to flood her memory

with him

he's never been too far away

to cross her path

bring her tears

like most men, he wouldn't understand

.　.　.

women cry in relief

release

to conjure, to caress a reminiscence

trapped in long ago

far away

gone

never forgotten

part of the song

made every sunrise

close to treasure

every sunset

unforgettable

as her life

her marriage

her children

without him

like most men, he would never understand

what she dreams of

why she cries

. . .

she is a woman

she knows

he would never have forgotten

she has had her husband

raised her children

seen suns rising and set

caught memories and the moonlight in her hair

how could he?

when she wears Je Reviens

at wrist and her throat (even now)

always and still

for him.

3

———

NATALIA

She wanted to be borne in mind as a fragrance

Having not been brought up to the idea of being beautiful

she was raised up to clean corners, light biscuits

and a grandmother's critical tongue

scornful, lip curled, lookin' her up and down

"Don't waste too much time on perfection, Girl

The Lord surely did not".

the smell of beeswax and condescension

laid heavy on her nostrils

except by herself, by her window

where rain-mist wound through magnolias

sent the drift of roses and lilacs into her dreams

so she would scrub elbows with harsh lemon and mint

spent any heartaches in magnolia showers

or a jasmine water-wash

Afternoon promenade 'round the little town square

the fellahs hoot-whistlin'-holler-"Hey Baby!
Come here, why doncha?"

They were after the hip-shakin'-flash-that-thigh gurrrl-you-know-you
see-him watchin'-at-chu (yeah, I do)
girls
rouged and sepia, hot brown sin

they never noticed her, except that

days or weeks or far-times later, they'd wake

itching and discontent

to hold that scent, to remember

even as old men, how they ached to hold onto

the grace

of that scent

     . . .

that scent that lay with them like loss

deviled them with could-have-been and lavender

riled their sleeping when breezes washed the hollow

She wanted to be borne in mind as a fragrance

so that when she finally took a lover

and one after that and one after him

she washed her hair in aloe

scrubbed heels and elbows with rain and green tea

drank rosewater and honey to sweeten her breath

they remembered, her lovers

the hip-switchin' fast gals

high yellas and ebony-cheeked hussies

trailin' seduction and store-bought sin

talkin'/ braggin'/ counted coup to each other

bold and hungry in sunlight

But she laid in their dreams

she was never a whole desire

just something sweet

"Soft, like light lays in a flower at dawn-time"

they'd murmur

praying a little when they got to be old men

that the scent would grace them one more time

disremembered her smile, her name

her lovers wanted the memory of the way she smelled

to embrace them one more time

She wanted to be borne in mind as a fragrance

and having never been brought up

to the notion that beauty will define itself

given enough time

she sacheted her head-scarf with

lily-of-the-valley and violets

linen water with lavender, freesia

took permanent residence on her skin

drank bergamot black tea

and wild peppermint to cool her breath

and frisk her blood

then settled at church with who had been those hip-switchin' hussies

quiet now, layin' low in flowered silk and fancy hats

scenting with vaseline and talcum powder

Men had caught the ones they wanted

still remembered smackin' lips

ebony-blush sin on the promenade

saffron babies switch-struttin' 'round town

flinging hips a little harder when the fellahs would

hoot-holler-c'mon baby-shout

one smile and a kiss (if you were wit' it, maybe you'd git it)

their houses smelt quite properly

of beeswax, vinegar, bleach

greens, lemon chess pie, catfish, burgoo

nostalgia and some a' blue regrets

if they twitched hips now

it was only to shift so their bones would settle right

Their daughters, not raised to the idea

of beauty in self realization

their sons, reared to hear a hip-shake

scent blush-red sin a mile away

sought her house on Wednesdays and Saturdays

baking days

their mothers made cookies, pies

but vanilla and brown-sugar sweet

ginger, cinnamon, small regrets and pumpkin spice

took permanent residence in her house

in the caress she gave each young cheek

warm nutmeg dusted inside the memories she hadn't planned for

because scent has no progeny

mists on rain and wind call no lullabies in their journey

shed no tears over first steps or forgotten fairytales

And she wanted to be remembered as a fragrance

the children called her Miz Used-Ta-Be

'cause the cookies tasted like

how their mamas said sweets used to taste

smelled of the olden ways

sugar sifted by hand, recipes known by heart

they slept with the taste of her traditions in their mouths

their fathers dreamt of her by

the memory of gardenias and aloe

by the memory of how a soft light will lay in flowers at dawn

She slept in the memory of vinegar and beeswax

her grandmother's voice

"Don't waste your time on perfection, Girl

The Lord surely did not."

set thorns inside her pillow

but her dreams spun magnolia

and wind-blown rose

sweet and wistful as hopes not meant to be realized

her hopes

She wanted to be borne in mind

as a fragrance

she wanted to be borne in mind

and having never known clear sight of her beauty

she waited

(always)

to be born.

4
___

TERESA

My mother taught me a thing or two

before she died

how to dress properly

how to clean a kitchen the way it's supposed to be cleaned

how to represent myself as a Black woman

she taught me how to recognize a lady

"This, she said, is the sort of person I want you to know,

the sort of person I want you to be."

to be that person, my mother's wish

it needs grace, wit, a rare, eternal elegance

a way in your world and walk that assures

passage to all others

"Beauty, she said, is never enough."

my mother taught me how to

recognize a woman of consequence

to be that person, my mother's wish

it needs strength, a quiet power

intelligence that burns, that questions

that survives

"Experience, she said, will never be enough."

I recognized you at once, Teresa

my mother trained me well

it's not just your beauty

and you are, undeniably,

beautiful

it's that rare, breathless elegance, that fire

the power of reminiscence in the stories you tell

the myths and magic of another world

that so captivate/reassure

your daughter and my sister

my mother burned me a few times

before she died

I don't think she meant to

within the realm of her generation

I was a threat to myself

"Security and marriage," she said

I do understand

she wanted me safe from my dreams

she fought like all the warriors of our bloodline

to keep me separate from the world

I need to breathe

you unconditionally believe in who I am

the art that let me be, lets me breathe

and that acceptance has been as loving and gracious and necessary

for me

as any lessons my mother taught

. . .

then again, you had the luxury of not having to raise me

I don't blame my mother for the way she felt, a lot of the things

she did

but I was rarely comfortable with her

I have known you for all of a year

we have spent only a very few hours

yet we laugh over joyfully common points

admit the absolute need of being open to whatever is possible

my mother thought my heartaches would cripple me

while you can catch the teardrops over past love

and help me know how to cherish the loves I'm crying for now

you miss him, I know

my sister's father, the husband you beguiled

and frustrated and must have amazed

"50 and more years, you don't know how I miss him", you said

I understand that, I do

the silences that lead you shouting for the Phillies, jumping and

waving your arms

just to fill all the lonely spaces of grown-up children

gone away husband, and a house never empty

I understand that, I do

it's the same reason I can never be without music for too long

in my head or under my hand

we both know, Teresa, that sound

for better or worse, carries its own passion

and our hearts require

in all its torrents

passion

I wish we had more time together

to meet and muse over tea and wine

kitchen tables or sunlit, musical terraces

you're funny, you make me laugh

I say things to you I could never have said to my mother

you answer me in ways that

(slightly) shock my sister, your daughter

she swears you would never say such things to her

she reflects you, you know

not just her beauty

and she is, undeniably,

beautiful

your lineage sings in her laugh

her eyes, her cheekbones, her fierce desire to hear and feel

every element of the world

her love of the life and a birthright

for a country from which she is banned

she owes that to you

my mother left me with a lot of

good things

not just jewelry and recipes

but a deep-seated faith in

accepting the true joys of my life

I don't think we ever saw joy the same way

that's alright

the faith is what's important

it led me straight to my sister, your daughter

it led me straight to you

rare and graceful and elegant

proud and powerful and fired with, tempered by

passionate, thirsting intelligence

it is not surprise that I love you

and I undeniably

do

how could I know any other way?

my mother trained me well.

5

CALLIE DANCED

Born in the night, she

the moon spinning crafts

in the deep red of bloodfall

or the most secret parts of a rose petal

air cold enough to burn glass

etched a hard memory into the

willows in the hollow

so hard a memory that they

shuddered to grow

for year til next year

elder ladies stood praying in corners

of the house

"Why don't you scream, Child?

Cry out,

it will ease the pain"

"Oh, why don't she scream?"

Callie's maman a-bed

walking the floor

drawing deep breaths of air

too warm from the big fire

one step, two

bit lip, hummed song

moaned low

like a woman brought to climax

she could

not delay

she would not scream, her

one step, two

bit lip, clutched shawl

walked the floor, drew warm-air breath

one step

two

Callie's maman called her name

Treasure Lucent, her

an island beauty, cat-green eye

against skin black-black velvet soft

a voice that called the nightingale to shame

she carry and smile of herself

like our Lord's most favorite daughter

around the town they whisper

"She a conjure-woman

such voice, such walk

like our Lord's most favorite daughter

those eyes so quiet and wise"

the elder ladies 'fraid to not come

help her in child-bed

'fraid not to speak even when she would not

Treasure Lucent had married a blues-man

Orpheus Danon, him

a pretty man with voice rare

and shamin' the angels

had kissed Treasure's hand in

the heat of that far gone-day

whispered love songs in her ear that night

and every other since

cinnamon skin, some Indian for high, proud cheekbones

and oh, he loved his Treasure

loved her into warmth and memories

and now this baby

this baby for whom Treasure Lucent

would not cry out

one step, two

clutch shawl, bite lip

one step, two

moan soft like a woman brought to climax

that cannot be delayed

outside, thunder shook and snow fell

outside the broken-glass air

shivered itself and clattered like a skeleton

Treasure sang one high, clear note of music

laid a-bed, bit lip

and Callie danced

danced out of her maman's dreams

and her daddy's desire

.   .   .

danced from between her maman's thighs

and laid, arms and legs waving

shaking, jumping

cried one high, perfect note of music

"A seizure" murmured the elder ladies

crossing themselves 'gainst the devil

"A baby born in seizure."

But Treasure smiled and knew

"My baby just reaching out to hear

everything

with toes, arms, feet

hear everything

it was her daddy's music and mine

brought her here, sent her

earth-bound

her daddy's music and mine

just layin' on of hands."

She hold that child light

hands poised, cat-green eyes fierce

the too big-fire beating heat over

black-black like velvet soft skin

and the old ladies said "God's blessing"

and beat feet to the village, them

and Callie-just born

Callie-fragile

Callie called by the music made

of her daddy and maman

Callie danced.

II

"That girl, that girl too different, she

that girl, that girl don't ever

still herself

that girl, she high-step float on air like it solid ground, her

that Callie Lucent-Danon

never still, her

her never work-weary or sit quiet."

"Her maman a conjure-woman"

whispered the elder ladies

"That why she never still

never

body silent.

And why she got that plain name, her?

How one Treasure and such man

as called Orpheus name their child

that plain name?"

Treasure Lucent was no conjure-woman

but her grandmere, Mathilde, had been

and she knew the importance, the way

of things

her say

"Callie plain-named because

you must not call magic things in

a complex way

lest they be misunderstood

and my Callie is a magic thing

the mingling of blood and music

and moon in willows

where the air snaps like broken glass

stand back and watch now

this magic is blood and bone and snow in the wind

watch this simple-name magic

lest it be

misunderstood."

.   .   .

and Callie-plain-named

free beauty like her maman

Callie, colored nutmeg and favored

half her daddy and half her

conjure-woman grandmere

Callie danced in the sun like stars

set the wind to wrap wings

around her body

set the stars to kiss each fingertip

the magnolias in the hollow

bent low and back, fell leaf and scent

into her hands

and

Callie danced.

III

Callie grew

touched skin and nerves, heart and heels

to each note of high, wild music

sung or spoken

took a lover, she

after Treasure and Orpheus had

been buried

       · · ·

they had fallen in love

kept falling til age and time slowed the step

took them both

Orpheus had kissed his Treasure's hand

that one far gone-day

wrapped them in love and memory

and all time

Callie listened to the moon, she

spun her daddy's notes into

her maman's memory of conjure-woman ways

and took a lover

a pretty man, him

walked like our Lord's favorite son

skin mahogany red, face drawn by a

fine-handed angel

featured like a star in winter

tempered proud--oh, my

smiled like a sinner knowin' preacher's secrets

eyes deep and quiet

temper crackled

like a fire set to willow wood

except to kiss Callie's hand

to warm her limbs and body and blood with him

brass bed deep, sweet, and soft

as the fire in the big room

beating heat on her cheekbones

and bare shoulders, skin nutmeg

and brown-sugar-sweet

Callie—hand-touched whisper quiet

Callie—kissed slow as snowfall among the magnolias

Callie danced

suspended air, tasted salt-sweat

shook limbs and lips and thighs

called high, clear notes--a woman

brought to climax

that cannot be delayed

over and ever again

chased the memories laid in

her daddy's music and nightingales put to shame

laid light, poised hands on her lover's shoulders

to pull his magic into her

deep as red in the blood of the moon

soft as the most secret parts of a rose

bit lip, hummed song, shivered hard

as cold, broken-glass air, reached out

for everything

never bothered to explain

one does not give magic things

complicated names

just said

"love"

to sunlight

and the stars at the tips of her fingers

said "Love" to the mahogany and fine-featured man

Callie Lucent-Danon

called conjure-woman kin

Callie—her maman and daddy's magic and music

Callie—for the rest of her life all through

Callie danced.

6

TANYA'S POEM (FOR TANYA RAZ)

She is joyful

the words tumble, fall, beat in

her brains and heart

without respite

they will not let her sleep

she is joyful

she is jubilant, she is proud

she is afraid

she cries because

the words will not let her sleep

and she is living between the

cross of music and lyric

.   .   .

she smiles, she feels Sarah and Bessie

has baptized herself in the

blood of my heritage

been blessed back into the grace of her own

heart/beats to Ibrahim and Gil Scott

the fire in every note La Caita throws

into the stars

she is at home among the universe

wanders nomad in and out of time

she is afraid

the world is moon and stars and open

a galaxy to command

and she feels vulnerable

and alone

she is wicked, seductive

tastes, teases the rhythm of words

and sound

luscious between her thighs

shakes beat-hot hip, licks syllables

with the tip of a siren's tongue

til it comes

exactly the way she wants

then pulls back, suddenly shy

and possessed of maiden's reticence

she does not understand

yet

that virginity

in this world

is never meant to be more than

fond reminiscence

you must immerse in

acquiesce to

this desire

she enjoys her solitude

craves the caress of

silence and quiet hours

she is happy, satisfied

living in her head

she is lonely

without the voices that

cheer her to acceptance of their love

she cannot breathe deep

without their presence

.   .   .

she is rejoicing

the images dance on the

feathertips of her fingers

she is powerful, beautiful

necessary

she is not sure

she cannot be reassured

I can only tell her

"Sweetheart, revel in this

the truth is never easy

Sweetheart, these tears are not transition

the bleeding will be eternal

a cascade of thorned roses

I'm sorry."

she shines too bright, too brilliantly

to make sense of what her life has become

it makes her angry, it makes her burn

it sings and plays and cajoles her

seduces her into not-by-chance encounters

other voices steal her time

. . .

beg for her words to explain what

they are forbidden

she is

honored by this

honored by the chance to loose fire

and truth in the name

of women she has only met between stanzas

she is humbled

she is tired

she wants the voices silent

but she cries when they stop

outside of her heartbeat

for even a moment

I tell her

"Baby, let it go

Baby, it's alright

it will be alright"

she is wild, beautiful existence

she is a woman

she needs to know

·   ·   ·

the tears are blessing

they prove she is finally free.

LYRIC II

LOVE

7

5:55

It's 5:55 a.m.

the numbers are imprinted on the insides of my eyelids

because looking at the cellphone flash hurts too much

so I pry it open just enough to see the time

just a trick of light

my eyes still burning

It's 5:55

I am thinking of you

brushing my hair, walking in what is still moonlight

before the first hint of a day I cannot share with you

anymore than I could share my nights with someone else

it's only an exaggeration to call you my every breath

if you're not

you cradle the cold shadows

mingle with fog and ragged shreds of moonlight

while I wait for a bus to my day's reality

It is still 5:55

and I am tasting your laugh on my fingertips

chancing a kiss onto my mouth

if you were really a gentleman, you'd never hold me close again

and time would stop standing still as the quiet stones on this street

and I

could move on

but it's 5:55 a.m.

and no matter how many hours I pretend to fly past

a dozen meetings and errands, the occasional meal

none of that matters

because the light and my heart woke me up this morning

both carried your name

everything in my life carries your name

and it hurt

it hurts

and people tend to record the hours of their pain

and it is now 5:55 a.m.

when your voice called me yours for the five hundredth and

fifty-fifth time since you ever said

"Hello"

to me

I only say your name in one of two ways

so people won't think I care

and whispered to myself after I come away from hearing

or seeing of/ about/ around you

The first is discretion, the second is because I am

greedy and selfish

and need to lick, sip, touch my tongue to every syllable

like it was the first snowflake

or a square of Belgian chocolate

They say when you are naming something or someone

to shout the name one hundred times

if you can still bear the sound of the syllables

the name must be correct

I have sung, shouted, laughed, whispered, ached

your name five hundred and fifty-five times in the last

splinter of the last millisecond

of any time-system my body and mind can recognize

in the milliseconds

between the call and response of

every synapse fired

in every stroke of the pen writing this poem

and I am not yet weary

of the way it weaves itself into my hair, around my fingers

into my blood and bone

because, as my girl Kaddara says,

this is not a love poem

I've only truly written three of those in my life

one to a man who wound his lies around my time

one for a man who sits every day at sunset

with his face to the wind

tells the sun to kiss my wrists and glance heat across my fingers

because he cannot

and

only once

to you

only once

because when you have said all there is to say

there is no need for repetition

I mark time in other ways now

in cliches of "never enough" and "too soon" and "it is so, so late"

you will never be too late for me

I lie down in softest scented linen

lie still to feel you wheeling and tumbling through my blood

lie quiet, lie still

others' days have ended and begun again

mine has not changed

I

will not change

You

are imprinted on the inside of my eyelids

a trick of light

that sometimes just hurts too much

I brush my cheek

and exhale the airs of your name

like snowflakes and Belgian chocolate

I pry my heart open just enough to see you and

It is 5

:55

a.m.

8

FOR….(I'LL LET YA KNOW)

I was born to this

born to spin words 'round the tips of my fingers

til your circulation stops

and rejuvenates itself into 24-7 heartaches that only serve to

clear your head

I was born from pure hope and golden dreams

that beggar any maharajah's imagination

and if I cannot be heard, it's only because

the wind in your heart

does not lie at my beck and call

.   .   .

(but it will)

I am the god-daughter of a field holler and the purity of notes

even Mahalia could only dream of

I cut my teeth in smoky bars, noisy coffee-houses, street corners,

and the whispering caress of angels' wings

I draw blood-scarlet tears when I have to

pulverize illusions into diamond

throw light upon a passing stranger's wistful desires

make sure that no single word dies from

not being honored

and I have spent tonight

with words and music that lifted me up

cut into my heart like fired glass

bored me to disgust or ennui

made me ache

all to say that

I was born to this

. . .

but I was also born

to be with you.

9

SEDUCTION

Come to bed, Love

my bed

tender and knowing

and ready

come to bed, Love

warm my sheets and my soul

cosset and comfort me

the morning is only as fierce

as we let it rage

draw the curtain

subdue the sunbursts in my eyes

kindle a different fire with the

feathertips of your fingers

so we can see each other's hunger

come into my bed, Love

tempt me, tease me, taste me

make me ache

for the sweetest miracle

let me surrender

draw your breath deep in my mouth

than lie back, lie still

I want your pleasure to be

complete

let yourself tremble

anticipating

the subtle gloss and suck

of my lips on your...

well...

you can choose the spot

Come, to bed, Love

my bed

talk to me

(just)

talk to me

make me laugh

dance your tongue-tip 'round

the shell of my ear, under my breast

across my stomach

whisper secrets and nonsense

light as a snowflake courts the petals of a winter rose

then taste, lick, sip

from my ....

well...

wherever you choose, Sweet

wherever I am warm or wet or

aching

with the glow of the morning

and your attentions

let me kiss you

let me arch my back

just enough to

make you bend to

my mouth

stroke the kindling spot

with your hand on mine

while you slide drops of warm moonlight

down my throat

let me taste, tease, lick

every path

every hollow

every

where

lie back, Darling

tell me what you need

let me bend just enough to

bend down

blow soft down

the length of

wherever you choose

let me sigh, Love

make me moan

hold my hand tightly enough

so that we can't let go

pull me into your forever

is right now

hold me tight

hold tight

pulse inside me

like a star

courting the tip of a candle's flame

one

breathe

two

breathe

one two, breathe soft

hush

hold tight

just please

hold

hold me tight

and come

to bed, Love

it's still morning

and the sun is

only a dove

courting the taste of a raindrop

bold and trembling

we'll make us

a miracle

laughing, aching

touching

with the feathertips of fingers

come to bed, Love

my bed

Now.

10

RACHEL'S SONG

Sometimes, you need a light

Not to linger near or beckon

or play guide

just the idea of one

something to promise clarity, at least

(a little hope

if you're lucky)

Sometimes, you could use a star

not to wish on or romance over

just

there

to remind you

that there are so many other mysteries

so much that is bigger and more brilliant

than

you

will ever be

And sometimes...

Well, that's the problem with it

sometimes are just that

some

times

minutes days

hours

something to record the steps of a heartbeat

we can't hold onto them

we can't bring them back

they're not dreams

you can always re-live

re-visit

a dream

Us, Love

we made

a dream

savored like drops of wine

on tongue, on fingers, on anxious lips

like the flash of bright copper in raindrops

or the touch of cool sheets on hot nights in the summer

So when you say

"we had some times"

I can't disagree or elaborate

I can only remind you

that we always

we are

(still)

meant to be

a dream

cherished and constant and ongoing

. . .

I couldn't ever give you some finite span

of

hours

minutes

days

I never thought we should settle for less than

forever

for less

than a dream

I don't want time to do it over

I don't want time to do it right

I want that infinite space to explore

and make beautiful

I want to live

in possibility

I have never wanted more time

with you

I want a dream

with you

to dream

with you

See, Honey

dreamers never learn "goodbye"

just

"I'll catch up"

or

"Don't worry, I'll wait for you"

because they know they won't spend

forever

just some

time

So...

I'll catch up

(or you can wander a few steps back)

You know, like

light

or a star

just so we know the other is somewhere

there

waiting

and that possibility is a thing

so much bigger and more brilliant

than ourselves

Just keep on moving, Honey

we'll take the dance at its own pace

we'll get us

right

where we should be

on the same plane

in the same sweet

peace

We'll be happy

some

time

wounded, bleeding

frail/flowers

some time

that's okay

.   .   .

It's only the steps of a heartbeat

minutes

hours

days

and we

(not all that long ago)

set our hearts

on

Dream.

11

———

TAKEN

It is a

sweet

brightness

softened by a

nomad's breeze

seductive

light of spiced apricot and golden dust

warm and sly as a whisper

I am lying in a gown of silk

scented with rosewater

and your promise

the light

deepens

the wind

shifts

I am

wet

and it is very hot

one hand trails along

the curve of my thigh

the other brushes my

lips

then beckons

to you

I lie halfway between

the world and a dream

the balance delicate as lace

one small sound will

destroy

or

confirm

the illusion

I'm not sure if I'm

dreaming

it doesn't matter

because you

are here

one finger travels along

the curve of my breast

one hand guides mine

to your

mouth

you lightly suck each

fingertip

then

brush my

lips

with yours

the kiss

is

seduction

bursts of light and fire

pulse honey-sweet

over my tongue

and into the

back of my

throat

the wind

changes

my gown is over

one

shoulder

and around your wrist

the light and my breathing

deepen

the kiss

deepens

the air is scented of tangerine

and cinnamon

.   .   .

the light

changes

and you are

inside

me

first with a kiss

then

you

are

inside

me

one hand strokes

my hair

the other traces the

echo

of our desire

along my heartbeat

pulsing in my throat

at my wrist

the curve of my thigh

between

my thighs

our rhythm

deepens

we are

wet

and

it is

very

hot

your kiss finds the

hollow

of my

throat

my hands trace the curve

of your back

the rhythm

deepens

my breath

quickens

the rhythm

changes

the light

moves

to cobalt

then quicksilver

the air

is scented

of sweat and

roses

we

inhale

tangerine

and cinnamon

the light

deepens

one hand trails the floor

the other traces

heat

along the curve of your

thigh

the wind

moves

I

scream

we

sigh

in tangerine and

roses

my gown is

under our heads

across my thighs

your mouth

whispers

on my breast

one kiss

we

kiss

your

hand strokes my

hair

we are

changed

.   .   .

and the wind

moves.

SANTIAGO...AND THE LADIES

For a while....longer than should have been...I adored someone who could charm the birds, etc. I wrote poems about the women he beguiled into his life, and then (foolishly) became one. I ended by making sure he left my life, but the poems were too good to throw away.

12

AN EASY TRUST

We have come to this point, Amor

to the point where it is time

to say all the truths of how we feel

the time needs to be gentle and true

and it has to be now

the words, our words, need to be gentle and sure and true

otherwise, we will never be able to see each other clearly

I want to hear you, Amor

I want to fold everything you say

soft around me like a warm fire

or the sky at sunset

or my dream of the perfect man

. . .

I want to hold you, hear you

bring your words to me as a child brings sugar to its mouth

You are so strong, so absolute in how you feel

how you love me

corazon, I wish I had that same strength

Por favor

will you please, Love

let me speak first

please, my heart beats too fast

I breathe my nerves

because I need to, have to

make you understand

so I can stop the thoughts, the doubts

pinching at me like a naughty child's fingers

or a vengeful rose

Amor

this is not an easy trust for me

listen to me

please

I trust you to hold my heart, I trust you with everything I have to give

but the journey has been slow and very painful

filled with lessons that shattered

bit by delicate bit

the woman who could have given you all

without reservation

All that you see, all that I say

is not just what has brought me to this point in my life

brought me to you

it is how I have survived til now

it is rough-edged,

shrill sometimes,

not beautiful

it is not that I can't help myself

I don't know if I should

I have no frame of reference for this love

Love, I am asking for patience

knowing that I have no right

I am asking for time

knowing that there may not be any left for us

I am asking you to hold faith in the way our eyes sing

our bodies ache

our souls embrace and dance like lovers in the square at midnight

fused together til even a drop of moonlight

cannot fall between

with him

love was measured in how many sacrifices I had to make

with you

it is counted in laughter and warm kisses

in tastes of wine from each other's fingertips

I am not used to, I am not sure

I can live up to this

I am afraid, sometimes, to believe

because before

what I knew in my soul

betrayed me

With him, I lived in the shadow of hard lessons and denial

other people ordered my destiny

.   .   .

Stand where you are, my light

clear, strong, radiant

hold your hand to me

sing so that I can hear you even when my eyes are burning

Yes, I could let you come to me

carry me

but, how then would I ever be able to walk as a free woman

into your arms?

The way I am, the things I live and say

the way of me

listen and take all of my journey into account

please, do not confuse the sinner with the sin

know that I am doing all in my power to make sure

that you are not sinned against

If you are objective in judging my sins, you can perhaps understand

but if you judge me

we are lost

and I do not ever want to be lost, lose myself

again

not even in your arms

.   .   .

I lost myself before

to husband and children and other people's demands

I cannot live there again

I want to live with you

love where you sing and throw light

where it is warm

where we are safe with each other

where we sip starlight from each other's lips

We are meant to drink from the wine of each other's hearts

but we must drink it all

moonlight and soft kisses

taste everything of honey

daylight sometimes touches the throat

not so sweetly

knowing that

let us empty the cup, Amor

til every sip is gone and remembered

Te amo, te adoro

I love you, I want you, I need you to

see me

I am walking to you on the golden road of a new love

but I am a new soul with tender feet

my fears are like rough pearls

I fall and tear my knees

my memories are bitter with blood and regret

they laugh and savage my eyes like cold wind

my tears fall like glass and diamonds

but I will not turn back

Just hold faith, Amor

I am coming, I will be there

I will let go of everything

and trust the hand you hold out to me

learn to trust myself, not be so afraid in the journey

We will learn, one from the other

and together

Just as one day, we will be the last dancers on the square at midnight

so much a part of each other that the shadows cry in defeat

so tightly joined that even a drop of moonlight

cannot fall between.

13
____

ELVIA

The square is waking up

noisy cars, animals, roses and serapes

(and darker things, perhaps)

for nosey turistas who mangle the language

with silly questions

the air is all of light and heat

the fountain has just begun to play with the butterflies

the priest and the birds both rose singing

for them

it is just another joyful day

I only imagine all this

I can't say that I've seen it

because

you choose that moment to

smile at me

and I become blind to everything

I can hear nothing but the sound of your hand

taking mine

The square at mid-day

is heat triumphant in its power to

make collars sticky

and rich men out of the peddlers selling ice cream and cerveza

The nosey turistas snap camera after camera

chattering how they'll brag to their friends back home

children toss pennies copper-bright with wishes

the sellers shout their wares

dust hangs in the air hazy and golden

like brushstrokes smudged by an angel's wing

the scent of oil and flowers is everywhere

I have been told

I could not say with any certainty

because you have chosen this moment

to smile at me

and oh, your smile

Querida

your smile is the flower that lies in the center of my heart

If I were a troubadour, I would sing of being your champion

how I would wear that smile as my shield

and ride out into the world to bring you diamonds

lie the song of a nightingale at your feet

balance the planets in the palm of my hand to make you laugh

whatever your will

I will

I would say that a thousand years would pass like

the flutter of a hummingbird

if every morning, every night

I could bend toward that smile

like the fire that warms my bones and blood

sip it like air or water

hold it between my hands like the first full rose of summer

.   .   .

I would say it is the sweet dance of a river

freed to meet the ocean

the last word from the pen of a poet who has always believed in love

that it is where starlight reaches down

and fire leaps to catch the kiss

But I am no troubadour

just the one who lives too many miles

away from you

I find my way by the memories of the last time

they shine like silver pennies in the road that brings me back again

to you

again

The square is darkening

music and color and magic draw cloaks made of shadow

around themselves

lie on the sidewalk and church steps

and in the sticky palms of children sleepy with the sun

and too much ice cream

The turistas have had one too many cervezas

taken too many pictures

they stumble toward cars and buses, chattering about how "real" it is

and comparing restaurants

they fall silent when the bells signal day's-end

it is the only sound they have truly heard all day

The air is still, the rose petals fall from the flower-sellers' cart

the birds and the priest fall fast and safely asleep

it has been just another joyous day for them

The musicians shake a few last notes from their violins and voices

just enough so that we can dance a moment longer

we kiss, say "good-bye"

and I watch you walk away

as if stars live under your feet

I throw a handful of copper pennies into the fountain

and watch the drops tumble like moonlight

my heart sweet as drops of honey and pearls in moonlight

we both turn around for one last wave good-bye

"Te amo, te adoro" lights the air around us like fireworks

That, I see

that, no one has to describe

only because

Querida

you choose that moment

to smile at me.

only because

Querida

you choose that moment

to smile at me.

14

MERMAID (FOR NANZ)

Long away and very far ago

I was a mermaid

dancing, flowing in and out of tides

and time

time meant nothing to me

mermaids are immortal

we are not held by anything

or anyone

It was never in me to wonder what charms or intoxications land held

I had the ocean as playground, as home, as lullaby

I held the waves at my beck and call

on sunny days and moon-swept nights, my sisters and I would sing wild and brave and sweet

on the rocks that disappeared at high tide

Los marineros always wanted to get closer

they were frustrated, dumbstruck, beguiled by our beauty

they tossed gold coins and flattery

then crossed themselves and ran like children if I smiled

Some were kind or curious

most wanted to own me

or capture, then show me off as a curiosity

or trophy

or an elusive dreaming

I would not be captured or changed

If they were truly unbearable, I would tell my father

then watch their ships pitch and drown in the wake of his temper

many a man ended clinging to the mast, begging the Virgin to
save him

my father did not care to see his daughters insulted

. . .

Over the days, some of the princes and wizards offered me the chance to walk

they meant it kindly, I'm sure

but I never wanted legs

Why?

when I could flow the waves and dance the sun and moon over my skin and hair

rest quiet in the shallows, counting stars on my fingers

I suppose they thought I was wanting or lonely

I was immortal, my joys were no temporary thing

those with spells and enchanted kisses never understood that

But there was one I remember

of all the centuries,

there was one

his voice was all of gold, honey and music

he was not afraid to come close

there was no possession in his eyes, no fear

just admiration

"Senorita", he said, "will you dine with me?

I believe the fish is very fresh today."

.   .   .

and I fell in love

blind to my father's warnings

because my heart told me I could trust him

his lips on my hand were softer than the sun and moon in my hair

instead of asking silly questions, he made me laugh

we wandered as far as water flowed

He understood that I was not jealous when the land required him

just lonely til he returned

he was not jealous or threatened

when I left the warm shallows where we fed each other red wine

and chocolates

where we made love

to swim deep and silent for hours

he understood the call in my blood

he understood me

and I loved him for that, and for the magic of his smile

So when he left me, I mourned

but he was mortal, and I had always known we could not be forever

my father held me while I cried

the seas were restless, uncertain, dangerous for the men on their
ships

who cried and begged to the Virgin

. . .

my father did not care for his daughter to be unhappy

Grief made me worn and vulnerable

so one day, I accepted a wish from a wizard, and became mortal

laid my new feet on dry land

my father was very angry

the seas tossed tsunami, the waves thrashed and fell like thunder

he bade me elsewhere til his anger cooled

So I walked mountains

learned the tyranny of walls

bore children flawed only by the fact of their mortality

But I could not stay away

and my father's temper cooled

so I ride the waves again

sun and moon soft on my skin and hair

The ocean is still home, playground, lullaby

most men do not understand

they toss gold or flattery

then turn and run when they see the ocean in my eyes

understand that I have no interest in being captured or changed

but you

you have a voice all of gold, honey and music

there is no possession or fear in your eyes

only admiration

you understand that I will always need to go away from the warmth
where we

laugh, drink red wine, feed each other chocolates

where we make love

to ride the waves

feel sun and sand on my skin and hair

you ask questions, you make me think

you make me laugh

you understand the call in my blood

you understand me

my heart tells me that I can

trust you

I am not sure how far we will wander

I do not know if the enchantment will last forever

when or if the wizard will return to reverse the spell

. . .

all I know is that the ocean and the grace of your heart

have made me immortal

this love is no temporary thing

Long ago from here

when you are forever away

and I have gone to live in my father's house again

after all else fails or fades

and I cannot remember or record a fall from this grace

I will remember the sound of your smile like gold and music

your kiss like honey

your eyes filled with nothing save passion

and admiration

I will remember that you never wanted to change me

I will feel you bring my hand to your lips and say

"Por favor, Senorita, will you dine with me?

I believe the fish is very, very fresh today".

15
____

ONLY A STEP

It is only a step, Querida

just one small advance toward

all that is new and precious

toward the hand that wants to hold you safe, hold you tight

for all the rest of your days

It is only a key, my Light

that will unlock every dream I have been keeping prisoner

every desire you have chased away from your soul

because it hurt too much to want, to need

with such passion

take it warm from the palm of my hand

I will help you find every door to which it answers

·   ·   ·

Trust me, Sweet

there is magic at the end of every journey we make together

Tesoro, it is simply a kiss

the kiss I have waited for all my life

the kiss that will rescue my princess from dragons

that steal her sleep, make her doubt herself

as the miracle that she is

I stand here, su caballero

travelling on the only quest that will make sense of

all my life

the journey to your arms

to that willing kiss

soft, gentle como la luna persigue las sombras

necessary and deep as truth/ as water/ as air

And the song, Corazon

the song is blessed by every lover who has ever given their soul

sprinkled with drops of moonlight

counted in every caress, every sweet silence

every flame of the candle that lives

only so that you might light it over and over again

in the way your lips release my name

Oh mi amor, if beauty were all I required

I should have been satisfied to walk beside you knowing nothing else

leaving after I had made you mine for a while

but your intelligence, your brilliance

the tilt of your head, the laugh that warms every corner of my reality

the passion of you

enchants me, enthralls me

I cannot break free, I do not want to

ever

leave

My own, I have been lost for such a long time

all that you are

has given me back the lover

I was always meant to be

I was only ever meant to reach that destiny with one person

You

It is all so simple

a step

a key

a star that we have all eternity to hold

between our hands

You have all eternity to hold every part of who I am

between your hands

but I know that real love cannot/will not

be rushed

like fine art or true beauty

it needs time

I have all the hours heaven holds

to carry starlight into your eyes

Baile a traves del cielo conmigo

we will make the stars smile

drink wine and laugh and chase dreams or dragons

as you wish

My hand, my heart, a life together

la decision te espera

be open, trust me

I promise, it is all so simple

just come to me, Corazon

it is only a step.

16

NIGHTINGALE (FOR SANTIAGO)

The others, they loved you like fire

fascination overcame the fear

they came close to warm their souls or bodies

fly into the sun of your wit and laughter and touch

they chose to believe they could not be Icarus

you never lied to them about the heat of your convictions

they left singed

forgetting that being burned had always been a possibility

I came to you quite warm enough already

they others, they loved you like a beautiful antique vase

they could burnish and brag about before company

stroke and run cool fingers over the surface

they expected you to be forever as the day you first kissed their
mouths

You never lied to them about who you had earned your need to be

you reminded them that you would never just say what they wanted
to hear

that truth sometimes broke them

marred the perfection

they found they had no further use for you

left feeling betrayed, injured by their expectations

I have no interest in flawless things

they bore me

I wanted to kiss every flaw, celebrate every frailty, try to understand

every misbegotten choice

that is part of what held me close to you

I loved you the way my rose petalled tea cup warmed into the center
of my hand

snug and certain

it was designed to be there

you were the flower that lay in the center of my heartbeat

Love, did you not see?

You were designed to be there

You were a good man

and I am a good woman

a very good woman

more realistic than to love you like some precious metal or fire or glass

I loved you like snow

that soft whir of a thousand singular points

a million singular miracles sailing along my fingers, melting into blood and bone

claiming my skin

melting sweet and pleasing on the tip of my tongue

I could have danced in you forever

I loved you in desire hot as the sands Shahrazad crossed

to tell one thousand and one stories to her prince

desire that curved and tasted and held fast

to every thought and smile

(Oh, my heart, that smile)

. . .

I loved you in the passion of the ways and hours

I satisfy the need, the craving in my soul

for my art

my words lie sure in the strength, in the fire, of that passion

my certainty lay in the strength of the passions I sang to you

I was never so simple that I craved only to wrap our passion
around your

tongue and thighs and backbone

I wanted to wind ourselves to each other's breathing, arms wrapped
around tears and joy and touching

knowing we rested sweet, rested safe

(Oh Love, you held me so safe)

so gently, so absolutely correct

I could never see you as anything but

who you truly are

The one designed to lie snug and certain

in the center of my heartbeat

The others, they loved you like diamonds

rare, perfect

in a world of men who weighed false

so able to be kind or funny or passionate

suitable to every occasion

You never lied to them about your tempers or tears

they never really allowed you to be human

they left feeling pressured by what they perceived as the impossibility

of hearing the way you do

insulted that you required they themselves shine as brightly as the

pictures of forever in their heads

Me, I've always been a sapphire sort of girl

multi-faceted, clear as light, complex as dreaming

my radiance completely evident

and I know that you were afraid for me

because your best true talent was giving all of your heart

and you had been led astray by other's uncertainties or

misconceptions

you did not want to see me hurt

Darling, that would never have happened unless I lied to

myself about what makes my heart sing to me

.   .   .

You could not cause me pain without my permission

Love

you should never have defined me in the framework of your

disappointments

You always trusted my words

trust what I say to you now

I never lied to you

I was never so far away that I couldn't take care of you

I never saw or celebrated you as anything but who you were

very simply, Darling

I did not change

the way I know, the things I feel

did not change

That sounds romantically ingenuous, I know

but I have not come this far in life

by not being able to recognize the promises I am able to keep

You were real to me

a good man

blessed to have been loved by a very good woman

who loved you like snow and sapphires

A very good woman

who only wanted to dance in

you

forever.

LYRIC III

PAIN AND POLITICS

17

BE MORE, BE BETTER (FOR SOFIA)

From the time I was a little girl

I heard two things

"Be more, be better"

whether it was dress/ behavior/ speech/ grades

whatever it was

as a girl, I was

expected to be more, be better

See, you were told boys could slough off

it was okay

'cause boys would be boys

But girls?

Girls had to be women, you weren't even given that choice

of an in-between

we had to know how to

take care/ be strong/

take care/ be present/

take care/ pull the race forward/

take care

be more

be better

all the time

I would have enjoyed hearing

at least once

"Be more about yourself"

"Be better about doing things for you"

I would have enjoyed hearing

at least once

"Be more appreciated"

"Be better about who you let into your heart

and your life

and your bed"

I would have appreciated hearing

just once

"You don't have to be more of anything

or better at everything.

You are a Black woman.

Let them come to you."

I don't see that happening anytime soon

and I am sorry/ to

I am sorry/ for

my little sisters

who grow up under the burden of

be more be better be more be better be more be better

because it's never going to be

for us

or

to us

We are/ world over/ centuries older

the hand that rocks the cradle

we are somewhere in the background

of every man

who has ever taken power

we are the strong ones

the unassailable ones

the ones who keep on going

keep on kicking

keep on ticking

keep on fighting

We have to do more, we have to be better

because the world collapses without us

We have to do more, we have to be better

because we know in our blood and bone

that civilization does not exist without us

we have to do more and be better

just to stay one step

behind

And all that "do more, be better"

guarantees nothing

we are still paid 69 cents on the dollar

we are still ignored as if we do not exist

in policy and opinion

.   .   .

When we are assertive

then we are bossy and aggressive

when we are demanding of our rights

we are unfeminine trouble-makers

When we, God forbid, express an opinion that does not

fall into lockstep with whatever the current thought and policy is

(never mind that said policy affects our health/ our rights/ our bodies)

we are called traitor

ingrate

bitch

and weak

We are none of those things

We are simply forever/ forever

trying

to be more

be better

be more

be better

be more
be better

be more

BE

better.

CALL ME MY NAME

I walked into a meeting

a few days ago

hung back

(introverts do not

walk up and mingle)

walked into the meeting-room

smiled

and began the

torture

of

introductions

the Brown and Black folks

repeated my name, smiled

gave their names

hugged "Nice to meet you"

"Me encanta, corazon"

all was mellow

One of the white women

stepped to me

(hold on, hold on

I know you think

you know what's coming

but I wasn't even ready for this)

She stepped to me, extended her hand

gave her name

I gave it back

said mine

smiled

said it clear, did not stutter, stammer, or whisper

She smiled again and called me

"Susan"

· · ·

I repeated my name

smiled again, and got

again

"Susan"

When I politely

gently

firmly

corrected her

I did not stutter, I did not stammer

I did not simper, whisper, or shy away

Her response was something I had heard of

but never had happen to me

what she said was

"Well, I can re-name you. That's okay."

and it wasn't a question

I had to sit and breathe

for a minute

I had to sit down/ breathe deep

and think for a minute

I had to sit down, breathe deep

think for a minute

and not follow my first inclination

which was to leap onto the conference table

take off my earrings

and see did my girlfriend have some Vaseline I could borrow

truly, I didn't know

whether to be more hurt, angry, or insulted

Because, here's the thing

I have spent all of my life

keeping level

or at least trying

I have spent all my life

advocating for knowing which

battles to fight

baptizing myself in the blood of reason

and urging others, by example,

to do the same

only to be betrayed

by all that time, all that

calm, all that "be reasonable"

when some white woman looked me dead in my face

and told me

"I can re-name you."

And no, she did not say it

like a joke, she did not

apologize, and make the correction

she did not excuse her offense/

bad manners/ abject ignorance

she said it as a fait accompli

she said it as if she owned the right not to be inconvenienced

she said I as if she owned the right to dishonor

the intention of my parents

who did not stutter, stammer, or mis-speak

when they gave me my name

and yes, it is a big deal

and yes, I still feel it

Feel the sting of her privilege

landing on who I am

I felt the condescension

I felt the dishonor to my ancestors

slaves whose true names were

changed to be made easier to bid

or forbid

dehumanize/ claim as property

easier to break

down

I remembered the stories of

Native elders sent to reservation schools

given other names to standardize/ demoralize/

erase history

train memory of life beginning

from when THEY said

bring them to a God that wanted them

humble and subservient

I saw the indescribable pain

in my friend Pablo's eyes

heard his voice shake

talking about being tied up and left in a closet for hours

slapped/ starved/ shamed

for being Brown children

who would not answer to their Anglo names in class

who called to each other in Spanish on the playground

they were told they would not fit in

were too stupid to learn, needed to be "normal"

had to erase heritage to be

given the right to exist

Family lineage/ pride/ honor of ancestors

part of who we are, how we came to be

dismissed/ thrown away/ ignored

beaten out of people

to make them humble

or less

or less dangerous

So yes, it was a very damn big deal

that this white woman said

"I can re-name you"

and walked away, laughing

I bet she didn't think about it for a second

let it cross her arrogant, privileged mind

slow her roll for a heartbeat

My standard threat to folks

who get on my nerves/ cause me pain

make me ache with wanting to hurt you

is "Keep it up.

I'll write a poem about you."

So,

here's your poem

I can't call your name

because I don't remember it

(how's that for irony)?

When you hear this

I want you offended

I want you embarrassed

yes, please, be sick at heart

I don't care if you didn't mean it

I don't care if you thought it was funny

I just

don't care

Don't even think about

coming to me, cheek and eyes

tear-stained

keep your fragility to yourself

I am out of forgiveness for that particular sin

wars have been fought over the right

the necessity, the honor

of wearing the names

our parents gave us

they did not stutter, stammer or

mis-speak

You had no right

So,

take your privilege

and your fragile feelings

and your "Susan"

fold them up real tight

and shove them hard, deep, and pointed

somewhere I can't be bothered to see your ignorance

running your mouth.

19
____

CASSANDRA

I don't know if you know

what it's like to feel this way

if I can make you understand

this cold/ dread fear

holding my heart

squeezing it hard

why I can't breathe right some days

I have lived in this skin a long time

60 years is a long time

and of course I've been afraid

I'm human

I'm Black

I'm a woman

there is an element of fear

built into all those names

but I expected to live with that

as the price of the ticket

as a fleeting discomfort

as Stevie sings "just an ordinary pain"

a thing that could be assuaged or solved

that would go away if I looked it in the eye

and forbade it take residence

there is no need to pretty it with poetic turn of phrase

most days, I am afraid

or fearful

or watching and suspicious

it is no fair thing to have your certainty stripped/ ripped

away

Listen to me

in 1963, at the 16th Street Baptist Church

four little Black girls died of being in Sunday school

I was 4 then

every Sunday was rose-pink dress

white gloves and patent-leather shoes

Sunday-school in the church basement

that could have been me

it is not something you tell a child

my parents never spoke about it

not in front of my sisters and me

I think because it could have been

their four little Black girls

and because the horror of it

was more than any parent/ anywhere

could take

I found out about it much later/ much older

I remember thinking

"It will never happen again"

It was never supposed to happen again

.   .   .

And then regime

fueled by racism and hate

carrying every human filth

Hell ever devised

was voted in by a bunch of over-entitled

lickspittle cowards

afraid of change

I cried for two days after the

"Election"

then I got mad and did what I could

to keep the world on proper course

I did what I know best

and I prayed

I prayed so hard

because in spite of all and everything

I still believe

I will always believe

But the evil kept coming

it got easier to be ignorant

to murder under a blue line

to put babies in cages/ to lie/ cheat/ steal/ actively perpetuate evil

and I would wake up shaking sometimes

so angry

but

I still woke up

I could still work

the twisting, haunted fear in my chest

still had no

permanent

home

In 2015, at the Charleston AME Church

9 Black folks were massacred

heads bent in prayer

they died of welcoming a stranger

to worship

It was not supposed to happen again

not in my lifetime

not dead for being Black/ taking granted that

sanctuary is safety

.   .   .

I was already living in shell-shock with most of the world

but this was personal

to me/ for me

It was not supposed to happen again

In 2016

Evil clenched hands tight 'round everyone's heart

Now, the night riders are rapists with rich families

whose sons think they should not be punished for desecrating

women's bodies under "just a little action"

In 2020, to be Black/ Brown/ Muslim/ and breathing

is an invitation to be detained/ arrested/ murdered

with impunity/ with immunity

here is abuse of LGBT bodies/ differently abled bodies/ abuse of
power

Babies in cages is just another Tuesday

In 2019, the night-riders ran the Supreme Court

now, they run the White House

they run and ruin the country

. . .

And my spirit is tired

sometimes I am so sick at heart that I cannot breathe

cannot take the uncertainty of leaving the house and remaining

unmolested

for even five minutes

feel as if the crosshairs of a thousand guns are permanently trained

on my back/ on my chest/ on my throat

My heart and my words are all I have ever been able to offer the

world

the price of the ticket

But one is dying by inches

and I struggle every day/ every hour

to make sure the other stays woke/ stays honest

stays strong/

stays clear

A lot of days

I just can't

No doubt you are expecting a neat and tidy end

to this poem

there is none

the fear still chokes me

the valley between my shoulder blades/ the hollow of my throat

still aches with a painful/ heartless anticipation

Not always

I am not always afraid

I am not always in despair

the dark evil hell-winds do not tempest without cease

but there is no clean air here

Every sanctioned murder

every sanctioned rape

every sanctioned/ excused

beating/ imprisonment/ torture

comes/ takes its place as

just another doorway to all the lower circles of Hell

just another newsbyte before dinner

just another Tuesday

There is no safety/ no sanctuary

I am forced to swallow

"It could have been me/

It can still be me"

I am forced to breathe

"It could have been me/

It can still be me"

Am forced to struggle making my voice do its work

make my soul stop shaking long enough to do my work

I am forced to breathe/ choking

WE are forced to breathe/ choking

there is no clean air in this place

Only a blood refrain that should never have been birthed

only our killing/ bitter knowing

It could have been me.

It can still be me.

20

DEAR WHITE PEOPLE

It has become

something of a trend

to call folks

(specifically, Anglo folks)

out

especially by

(though not exclusively by)

Artists

Not in an evil or angry way

just in a Jesus-Christ-here-are-the-rules-read-them-this-time

sort of way

.   .   .

Now, I have never been one

to follow a trend

and I can gratefully say

that I love and am loved by

NPOCs

However

for those of you who still are not paying attention

for those of you sitting in the back of the classroom

scratching yourself and playing on your cellphones

for those of you responsible for at least

25% of my acid reflux problem

here we go

(and Jesus Christ, pay attention this time)

Dear white people

first, let's review the basics

don't touch my hair

don't touch my hair

don't touch my hair

however it waves, moves, weaves

curls, braids, or carries pretty, shiny things

sure

let your eyes be seduced

but keep your hands to yourself

in the words of one sistah on my Facebook stream

"my head is not a damn petting zoo"

and by the way,

if I have chosen to wear it pressed, straight, and unadorned

please refrain from telling me how cute you think I would look

if I let my hair go back to the motherland

Dear white people

I wear my clothes because I like my clothes

please stop trying to tell me

I need to garb myself in the old ways

that my swag and style need to be more about my homeland

(read your anthropology and then we'll talk, okay?)

Please do not take it upon yourself to point out

that my tastes do not run along "party lines"

do not raise eyebrow or deride my choices

in food, reading material, or music

I am grown and free

which means you may keep your opinions

to your damn self

Dear white people

I personally do not care

how you dress, talk, walk, or embrace the power of music

we all know the difference between homage and appropriation

so no matter how culturally light-fingered you are

please know you cannot out-hip me

I've been Black longer than you

Quick note: if you refer to your Black and Brown friends

as "your Black and Brown friends"

then you have no Black or Brown friends

And please

for the love of all that is

sweet, good, and holy

stop asking me how much I loved "Black Panther"

didn't go, won't be watching

(see next poem)

don't tell me how "The Help" "The Green Book" and "Black Like Me"

really opened your eyes to the reality of being Black

when the truth is all it did was make you happy to not be me and give you another hero (*translation: one who does not know what*

a good ally does) to sing praises over showin' us poor, ig'nant child-

like creatures the light and the way

By the way,

please stop asking me to perform at "Let's showcase the famous/

approved ones listen-to-them-sing-watch-them-dance and feel all

warm and fuzzy about Martin and Harriet Tubman"

otherwise known as Corporate Black History Month

one afternoon of soul food in the cafeteria and learning the words to

"Lift Ev'ry Voice and Sing" does not bathe you in the blood of the

struggle

Acceptance is not spelled "I treat you just the same as I would treat

normal people"

Please

stop telling me upon meeting me

"I believe there's only one race.... the human race"

and glancing proudly about applause and affirmation

I believe fairies dance on the lawn at full moon's light

that doesn't mean it's true

·   ·   ·

We no longer honor "they're old"

"I didn't mean anything by it"

or (my personal favorite)

"But *(insert the name of your Black childhood point of reference*

here) always thought it was funny."

And for the sake of seeing your children's children

grow and celebrate our wonderful quilt of diversity, I beg you

erase "Well, you're not like Kendra or Kevin or Toni at..."

(insert your point of contact with the only Black person you

acknowledge on a regular basis here)

"I can say anything to them and they know how I mean it."

My name is not Rosetta Stone

I don't do translations

For the uninformed, I will not be amused by jokes about

watermelon and friend chicken

I will not think big lips and a 'fro drawn onto a box of grits

is a fabulous gag gift

I will never be flattered by hearing "You're so much nicer than the

niggers at home"

. . .

Dear white people

let's not play "the police were in fear of their lives"

"that teacher was just being creative with her lesson plan"

"the border patrol and ICE are just doing their jobs" and

"the President isn't always racist, homophobic, and wrong"

Because, no, they weren't

no, she wasn't

no, they aren't

and, yes, he is

I am not charged with caring what you think or making sure you're

comfortable

So please, do not reference me as "sister", "auntie", or "nana"

without my specific permission

those liberties carry an historical charge that may well blow your

head off

You do not now, nor will you ever

have my permission to use the "n" word

in any way

shape

form

or configuration

"Well, I didn't mean YOU"

does not/ will not

save you

Use your common sense

open your eyes and ears to

the courses of the world

learn what things mean

don't talk

listen

you can't empathize

you may not excuse or be excused

Stop trampling over people's souls in the mad rush to say we're all

the same

Breathe deep

educate yourselves

watch your mouth

stop relying on what's familiar

to equip or bail you out

of uncomfortable times and places

And for the last

FREAKIN' time

Don't touch my hair.

21

FOR JACQUELINE PENHOS (WOMEN'S MARCH 2017)

"I wanted to go...but life got in the way...and I had to work"

We march everyday/

we march to work/ to school/ back home/ again/

march the 1,001 steps between kitchen/ and kisses goodnight/ and

homework/ and men/ and mama and daddy and church/ and the

club/

we march everyday/

singing and crying and holding hands/ and healing hearts/ we raise

our voices/ to the sky/ to our Lord/

to shout/

to praise/

to ask questions/

to make answers/ to make a way/

we march/ we make a change/

we change/

everything.

22

LOUISIANA BAPTISM

I got baptized in Louisiana

Sunday school teachin'/ white glove wearin'/

daughter of a gospel man

and I had been to the water

but never baptized til then

now, Baton Rouge is a pretty city

nice people, great food

down-home-South, where the men are to die for

and the women do their hair

Baton Rouge is a pretty place

trees and flowers and all around you

Water

whispering, beckoning

still

like ghosts or bad luck

now, I'm a sand and beaches girl

saw all that water, and decided on

total immersion

decided to wash myself clean

in a new moment/ new passion

new possibility

and I studied that water

gazed for hours, dipped my fingers

counted swamp stumps, watched mute as it fell and fell

from the bluest sky (save one)

that I have ever seen

I clenched my courage beneath my teeth

opened my arms

and begged to be received

The preacher man was called Time

wrinkled ashen with the strength of centuries

and fear and pride and salvation

I gave myself over to his brace on my back and shoulders

and he laid me down in water black as stolen jewels

black as a fiddler with bad intentions

black as a demon's wedding flowers

into my sister's death by stroke and stubborn

I was glad for it

she wouldn't have wanted to live anymore

that way

I ached because of it

because my nephews bled tears

I bled memories

most of them about what a pretty baby she'd been

what a brilliant beauty she'd become

her passing didn't make me want to go

just put me in slow shock and lagging pain and

glad she had

gone on

Time brought me up to breathe

sable bands at wrist and throat

bid the choir on shore sing

"Pass me not, o' gentle Savior"

and he did lay me down

in water red as bloody sunsets

water red as a lying whore's mouth

water red like sick and leaking fire

sharks swam in that water

carrion dived for my time/ talent/ soul

counted coup in illness and betrayal of trust and

promises made that weren't ever going to be kept

promises I was stupid and loyal enough to believe

washed away in cold, foul, bitter water

that tore over my skin and heart

like a sludge of sand and burnt sugar

Time brought me up to choke on clean air

choke on hope and wishes

Time brought me up to confess all and anything I had

not said before

and laid me down for the third and last time

in water moving so fast that houses buckled

lives were razed

and thrown aside like trash

Water gray as unwanted destiny

Water gray as diamonds losing their only light

Water infecting and filthy and dangerous

moving/ killing/ destroying

taking away any last innocence of 15 years

furnishings, trinkets

my best friend

15 years

not just damaged

destroyed

by the power of hard rain with no thought

but to demand cleansing

Time raised me up

called me daughter

marked me with a kiss

that infected my leg and robbed me of clear eyesight

shook my heart into something that drifts on the wind

and will not come home

(not yet)

I came back washed in water colored like blood and fear

black with loss

black like dying stars and burned promises

infected and hopeless

Time baptized and delivered me here to heal

the sun remembers my name

but not my face

not yet

I am still helplessly in love

with sand and beaches

but I shiver sick

just a little

shiver sick and cold and terrified

just

a little

whenever a hard rain

comes down.

23

SONG FOR MARTHA SULLIVAN (AND GRETA THUNBERG)

The world is not fond of prophets

a hard job, somebody has to tell the truth

about the way we live

the things we do

the wrongs committed in the name of

"It will turn out all right"

and those who raise up their voices to say

"Wait"

"Think"

"This is not the way"

are either vilified or deified

. . .

but never listened to

after all, one only gets 15 minutes to be heard

to make voices/ choices matter

any persistence beyond that point

is called pride/ arrogance/ need for attention

but no one takes it seriously

so the call or voice or warning

goes unheard, unappreciated til it is too late

and then we wail and cry for the old ways

for the safe times

for a prophet to solve all of our problems

we promise to listen this time

and the cycle repeats, spinning truth and reason into

the eye of an ever-vicious storm

the rains will never stop

the sun will hide its head away until we trust

until we listen

until the call for action is

synonymous with the call for believing in something more

than popular thought, widely held opinion

the vanity of hopes and dreams with no foundation of hard work

to hold them steady

the truth of the matter is

change is never made by prophecy

it just gives us the chance to try

before time falls in on us

and however or whatever you may believe

or believe in

the road is never different

yes, someone has to tell the truth

with no promise of ease, of comfort

with no guarantee that the world will ever take heed

no prophet ever survived a journey

armed with more than fewer of the shackles

the rest of us wear in resignation or ignorance or pain

.   .   .

and that one truth promises

that, difficulty or disdain aside

there will always be one to say what needs to be said

one who can live no other way

and that is enough

for hope.

24

SISTAHSONG (FOR STACEY ABRAMS)

I am a sistah to my soul

and a danger to those who cannot see past the lies created by their

history

I am a woman of color in a place that has dismissed, vilified,

made dangerous

the roads I walk

and ignored the path I make for the rest of the world

I hurt on my own time, I cry in shadows

because I have things to do

.   .   .

like nothing

but triumph forever

because I know how to

push back

push back

push back

I don't have time for threats

I make promises

so you better step, run, hide

messin' with me and mine

you better step, run, fly

messin' with the world

we are

bleeding

to hold together

you better run, fly, disappear

when we start using all of everything we have

inside

stories/ spirit-calls/

songs

I might cry in shadows, but I bring my sword/ shield/ battle-plan

into the light

so do right

or get gone

because I am a sistah to my soul

and I got things to do

and I know how to

push back

push back

push back.

25

ELEGY

You died today

it was

unexpected

I had seen the infection

possessing you for

some time

I didn't know it was so strong

I am invisible

you can't hear me anymore

you might catch a brief glimpse

as I shuttle from room to room

to avoid being seen

or heard

or imagined

where my heart should be is

a hole filled with

smoking ashes

and bad dreams

you died

and I became a ghost

that haunts the hallway

in a place that is no longer home for me

our father raised us to work

to be of excellence

to always stick together

"You will always have your sister"

he said

he lied

because you died today

that man appeals to the

worst of you

the hubris, the laziness

the belief that ease

will rain down and save you

from being miserable

I watched him turn you weak

I watched him make not trying

just wanting and hoping

easy for you

I watched him make you forget whose blood you hold

was it that much of a struggle

to work, to hold your head up

to push?

I know Daddy ran us hard, expected the world

I know sometimes it felt rough

but he loved us

was gentle when and where it mattered most

and I can't forgive you forgetting

his lessons

and it isn't that the infection was all that strong

just stronger than you felt like being

stronger than how we were supposed to

take care of each other

it killed you, killed us, killed every wish I have ever had

to be like you

do you understand I went into debt

to help you?

borrowed money against money I didn't have

to keep food in your mouth

went without things I wanted, needed

and bent over backward to make sure

you never

never

had to ask

do you understand that I was glad to do that

because you're my big sister

you danced on the moon for me

sent the stars down to take tea in our backyard

you taught me reading and boys and enough sense

to make sense of myself

when I couldn't

see myself

how can you not be the person anymore?

.   .   .

We were brought up to know

family is everything

family is everything

family is everything

Daddy said "Your mother and I will pass

but you will always have your sister"

Daddy promised "you will always have your sister"

and you died

you chose him over me

you chose him over blood

our blood

you died right in front of me

so cover the grave over

with a bier of thorns

scatter rose petals between the spikes and the coffin

and let loose one star-white dove

to carry my tears and memories to

a cleaner place than where you left me bleeding

I won't be there

I hate funerals

and I cannot forgive you

I will not forgive you

you bound my wrists, slit my throat

let the blood cascade over

most of what I've ever believed in

stopped me breathing

and you died

So, cover the grave over

with a bier of thorns

sprinkle rose petals between the spikes and coffin

I won't be there

I am a ghost

where my heart should be

where you should be

is a hole filled

with smoking ashes and bad dreams

you bound my wrists, slit my throat

and let our blood cascade over our father's promise

and I will not forgive you

you died

and I cannot forgive you.

26

WHAT ABOUT WAKANDA

This will not be a popular poem

so y'all might as well

just get ready

some of y'all will holler

some of y'all are gonna wanna fight

some of y'all will just bend your head and shake

"Lawd ha' mercy on that chile"

and all I'm gonna say is

"Don't start none, won't be none"

'Cause don't none of y'all sign my checks

or pay my bills

and even if you do or did

I have a right not to run

with the crowd

We're bad about that sometimes

Black people

wanting everybody to toe the party line

so just hold on, be mellow

and breathe deep

(you can hold prayer meetin'

for me afterwards)

I did not see "Black Panther"

didn't want to

will not be

(I will pause here for a moment

whilst y'all gather yourselves)

To quote the schoolyard retort

"I said it, I meant it

I'm here to represent it"

(haven't read any of the Harry Potter books, either

but that's another story)

It is not that I don't understand or disagree with the premise

it's not about the acting/ writing/ dream-making involved

I'm glad folks got paid

I'm sure it was visually stunning

I know it broke ground

I absolutely agree that the Academy choosing

"The Green Book"

to win anything but total contempt

was insulting and insane

I'm simply not all that fond of fantasy

and that's all "Black Panther" is

a well-written, beautifully filmed

dangerous

fantasy

Folks flocked to that movie

like they'd been promised the Second Coming

and doughnuts afterward

.   .   .

I saw an easy seduction

I saw too many Black people

decide and declare it as

a reason to be strong and proud and independent

Since when has coulda shoulda woulda

made this country anything better for us?

I saw too many Black people

adopt the idea of Wakanda as

new savior, new validation

a new way to make them hold up their heads

and straighten their backs

That should have been happening already

that image of yourself

of who you are

should have been in place already

One Black superhero did not

keep one Black man

from being lynched a few days back

terrorised and beaten the "old-fashioned way"

I'm sure the thought of "Wakanda" did not ease his pain

One Black superhero does not

stop us being murdered with impunity

It has not stopped the outrage of

white authority shaming Black bodies

it has not stopped, denied, or changed the

root of our experience in this country

all it has given us is a fairytale

and we have had enough of those

handed to us as birthright

you know, the ones about equality

the ones about judgement by character, not color

the one about how, with time and intelligence

racism would be erased in your lifetime

Is that the reality of any Black person hearing/

seeing/ reading this poem?

No

And I'm not saying the idea of such sanctuary

is not seductive

does not call powerfully in the blood

but the fact is

it's only fancy

You may argue that it brought you a sense of commitment

to love and family,

showed you how fierce and fantastic we can be

but if your daughters did not already know

that they are true warriors by birthright

then you are wrong

if your sons did not already know

that real men are about

grace, honor, and conscience

then you are wrong

If your partner did not already know

that you carry their heart more precious than a

motherlode of vibranium

that you will fight to the blood

to protect that love

then you are wrong

no comic book country and its inhabitants should have had

to tell you those things

My father was raised up in Jim Crow

fought combat for a country that did not

love him back

saved lives, understood art and honor

swore roses died of shame to look at my mother

and ever think they were beautiful

He held it down for his daughters, his grandsons, his woman

and never once heard the word "Wakanda"

My mother was raised up a Black woman

of intelligence, beauty, and far-sight

and that is dangerous in any era

she worked, raised five Black women with husband and certainty
often away

kept home and us together, loved books and design

danced alone to Motown while my father was at war

and lit up like glow of daybreak at the mere mention of his name

She held it down for her daughters, her grandsons, her man

and never once heard the word "Wakanda"

.   .   .

They raised up five daring/ dedicated/ dangerous/ delicious

"Don't you drop til you die"

Warrior Women

Where is their movie?

where is the movie for those who never once

relied on fiction to tell their worth

to work real dreams

did not find their faith

in a fantasy?

I'm all for beautiful ideas

all for inspiration

and I have nothing but respect

for the actors/ writers/ dream-makers involved

I'm glad they got paid

But Wakanda is not our saving grace

and nothing will make that stop being so.

27

WARRING-SONG

Night polishes my shield

the stars burn hard and unforgiving along

the names of warriors past

etched deep in the metal

there are none here who shun compromise

but neither do they hold back when

compromise is given no space to take root

these names are the names of women

these names are the names of men

.   .   .

these names are the names that burr/ glide/ scream/ sigh/

across tongues who only want to know

one way of language

one way to sing

but will not understand that there lies no art

in either

my people fought and told stories

warred and birthed music

innovated — taught — dared

the fools who disdain the bounty they gifted the world

will suffer for it

some weaponed with guns, some with fire, some with

ideas and knowledge crucial as raindrops to a land

parched by season

or terror

my weapon of choice is the word

· · ·

The word that can sway heart, call a lover

make a mind reach out, gasping, for just one more breath

it is sharp and merciless as sapphires

it is kept close as the color of my skin

it knows the name of every woman

it knows the name of every man

and says them all in prayer

at every hour

where I am either marking change

or preparing for war.

LYRIC IV

THE LILT AND LYRICS

28

FLOW (FOR JACQUELINE HILL)

Girl

you got this

you got this

Voice

begging to be borne on the wind

needing to be out defining new parameters and making

magic

you got this Will

that time and tears have attempted to break

(you can't be broken)

that's been trampled like a diamond in the dust

pick it up, dust it off

start a fire from all the thousand shining facets

You don't wait on easy

or convenient

or if/ when/ wonder

you run

you fly

Now

you sing

Loud

and if they can't keep pace

that's too bad

but you don't fold your wings and drag feet

for a

ny

bod

y

Folks better pray up and come on

'cause you got this

this insistent ringing in your heart

from the ancestors

urging/ demanding

you tell your story the best way you know

the only way it can be told

with heart

with honor

with an ineffable sense of being

with love

And a lot of folks won't like it

won't care

can't get it

that is not your concern

you may pity them (Girl, you don't have that kind of time)

you may scorn (Girl, you don't have that kind of heart)

You can only do service to the world

by being faithful with yourself

true

with yourself

sing the songs honestly

don't you shape those notes for safety

shape them for celebration

shape them for risk

shape them for prophecy

Folks better just pray up

get

right

and

hold

on

'Cause, Girl

you got this

this vision

Run

paint the sky and the wind

with words

NO thing

NO body

can destroy/ ignore/ alter/ deny

and step sweet and look good while you do it

('cause you know that's how we roll)

Pain?

oh yes

Doubt?

believe it

Insecure confusions?

yes indeed

all those right there

Nights when fear makes your mind freeze

days when the words mock you from a haven

just beyond the reach of your fingertips

when Frustration nags at you like a bitter old auntie

who has no friends and your cellphone number

Breathe

Pray

Dance

Eat dark chocolate with almonds

Make love

.   .   .

whatever it takes, whatever works

to remind you that denial of your tales and talent

is not known in the grand scheme of things

You can get weary

but don't get lost

You can get mad/ crazy/ disgusted

but you don't quit/ get lazy/ lose focus

or fire

Breathe

Love

take it al-l-l-l-l

in stride

and step sweet and look good while you're doing it

'cause you know that's how we roll

Girl

You

GOT

this

.   .   .

This way to redefine the world

and the words

Sing

Risk

run with all of it

FLY

and never forget the way and will

of the thousands women before

the way and will of the five thousands coming

are sweetening the road beneath your feet

and the wind at your back

all of us praying/ crying/ cheering you forward

praying/ singing/ shouting one single, sacred phrase

"Go, just go

just go

ON"

'Cause, Girl

You got this.

29

FOLLOW ME ON THIS

Poet

one who says, pushes, creates

sober, honest times

sweet intentions

One who brings your dreams free

lets you, makes you

tell the truth

I came to be

in the space between my father's smile

and my mother's grace

raised to honor, raised to respect

raised to know that God's right hand

rested lightly on my heart

my mother's history and hands rested

not so gently on my butt

when I did not come correct

it is how I learned to be correct

4 sisters, good grades, slumber parties

playing school and house and recording studio

cooking and church

I was a Dyson girl

I AM a Dyson girl

and my father loved me

my parents raised me with the sense to know myself

the sense to be myself

the sense of a necessary existence

I had the best childhood

faith and family and books

and so much music

there was always

music

"Now I lay me down to sleep" was my thank-you

was my "Good job, Lord

keep it up!"

I never fell asleep unsure

I never woke up wondering why

about my place in the world

the space between grace and love

I lived there

through moving and boys and discovering

well, acknowledging

that words took their breath in the feathertips of my fingers

took flight on my exhale

left mark and magic in the world

Follow me on this

the space between poetry and music is artificial

it does not exist

every poem I wrote/ will ever write

is anthem/ or ballad/ or lullaby

I truly do not know the difference

I could not/

cannot

see the difference

I do not see the need

it is all

music

and so

I sang

I knew I was born to sing

20s and 30s,

folks heard me

I made myself heard

a Black woman pushed by her ancestors

schooled by/ fueled by

the voices of women in flight

in my blood and bones,

in transition

.   .   .

I collected/ I drank

their voices

and sweetly rested each night

in the palm of the Lord's right hand

You know what's coming, right?

Life is not unfair, simply balanced

pain lies/ snickering/

in wait

I hit 40

my mother hit cancer

and was defeated for the first time I had ever seen

I took care of her while she died

and when she couldn't hit back that one last time

I stood at her grave, dry-eyed and shoulders back

my mother left me in the space between her memory and

full knowledge of the work left to be done

I still sang

had you known my mother, you would understand

I did not dare otherwise

Poetry

that which is made to breathe

by being passed into the hands and hearts of

flame-keepers and fire-singers

who will cradle/ love/ defend

the integrity of sound

and the light upon which it travels

I did my work

I travelled and taught

I found and fired other women to do their work

their words

In the space between

love come away here

love never come back again

Follow me on this

see, I didn't just work

I worked it on out

.   .   .

Okay?

And yes, I fell and bloodied my knees on the diamonds

love sprinkles at your feet

discovered it's okay to break your heart over life

you just don't break your back

lose your faith

because you have to move

work it on out

okay?

there was always work

always so

much

music

I felt/ I flew/ I lived

that sense of triumph/

of glory/

can intoxicate

.   .   .

You know what's coming

right?

I didn't

my father died

and I fell/ shaking/

into the space between certainty and pain

so acrid, so bitter and unforgiving

that it was years

two long

desperate

years

til I remembered who I was born to be

whose hand rested so firmly on my heart

had you known my father

you would understand

that I did not dare otherwise

Poet

one who exists in the space between rhythm and clues/ dark

chocolate blues/

sober honesty

who challenges daring out of pain

passing chance to triumph

works to work it on out

Follow me on this

the truths that created me rest in this hand

the truths I can and have and will create

triumph

dance

in the other

the fire

the voices

the words

echo loud and persistent in every chamber of my heart and
exhalation

I am a poet

I live in the space

between.

30

JENNIFER'S ROSE

A very sweet, very beautiful Asian girl

gave me a rose

in a rain-soaked afternoon of red-gold-jade silk

and dragons...

no, let me try again

this is too important

I'm not clear, not being clear

See, I've been doing this for a long time

and for the last few months

I've been wondering why

.   .   .

I've been struggling for the last few months

money has been too tight

heart and body too completely neglected

a fine case of exhaustion

a handful of very bad dreams

that fill the spaces where I could rest

echo razor-sharp and burning

during the day

a depression deep enough to be painful

but not dark enough to fuss about

all from the usual

teaching/ coaching/ making words

pushing/ shaping/ making words

creating/ breathing/ making words

for meetings and grants

making words for everyone but myself

I've been trying to remember

why we do this

carry the heart of the word bound to us

like breathing

or prayer

.   .   .

Don't get me wrong

money is lovely

and artists need to be paid

but it's not ever about the money

it can't be

and yes, we live on applause

poets live on recognition and applause

and anyone who says they don't is lying

But it's not that way, either

The rose is in my backpack for a couple of reasons

I have no vase for it where I sleep

the people I live with do not understand

my life or the demands of my schedule

they would only see it as they see me

irrelevant clutter

I will not make room for beauty in a place

where I don't want to be

 but mostly

it's there to remind me of why

we do this

because Jennifer came up the second day of class

to share a poem that was not on the assignment sheet

and I could have warmed my hands at the light in her eyes

that said she knew it was good

I could have fired my soul

with the passion to honor the word in the way she sang it to me

I could have given ease to the hearts of a million poets who had toiled

themselves into obscurity

just by recording her smile

when I told her it was one of the best I'd ever heard

And quite honestly, that would have been

enough to give me back my faith

but months later, at a New Year's festival

'midst firecrackers and silk dragons

this very sweet, very beautiful girl

who thought I would not remember her

hugged me, introduced me to her grandmother and friends

then disappeared into the crowd

only to find me an hour later

and put a very sweet, very beautiful

wine-dark rose into my hand

"This is for you.

Thank you."

I did not cry

(well, not right away

or for very long)

Mostly, I walked around for the rest of my busy day

the petals whispering on my cheek, fingers caressing the stem

through coaching and teaching and making words

through creating and breathing

and helping other people make words

for themselves

finally, ready to fall asleep,

I left my backpack open and close to my bed

so I could see it, touch it when I woke up in the night

The petals are drying out now

nestled soft with notebooks and pens, day-minders

the scent fading grace into

where I carry most of my life

The wine-dark red petals are drying out, failing

I pluck them one by one

out of bus schedules, from between book pages

brush them off and away from my pens and perfume

let them lie til they're dust and memory

to remind me of why I do this

why we do this

We do it because we have to know

the words will live protected, cherished

be the passion-light in hearts too young to realize til

just that moment

how necessary they are, how much we depend on them

to pay it

play it

forward

We do it because

in the end

the sound of our voices, the fall of dollars into our bank accounts

the applause

truly will not matter

we do it for love, because we cannot breathe otherwise

we do it to make life a bit more graceful

a little more important

we do it

for Jennifer's rose.

31

ON VIEWING A GALLERY PIECE

Is this how it ends, do you think?

A giant hand poses itself with a tube and

petulantly sucks the hours and miracles of lifetimes

into a sterile, airtight bag

to be held tightly closed for a thousand thousand years

lest they spoil

again

God holds hand over the earth

flicking the imperfect beauty of the world aside

like a pastry chef dissatisfied

with what seems so sweet and real to the rest of us

wanting to smooth the icing bland

clear

to start over

I can't believe that

believe in the possibility of anonymous expulsion

believe I'm just another thousand thousandth

of the heartbeat

I'm a Black woman, I want a show

I'm a poet

I need the lyricism of angels' wings

fluttering in 6-part music

I'm human

and arrogant enough to be disappointed by my whimsy

The last Doomsday call made me laugh

I told folks my version of preparation for the final end

was to eat a gallon of French silk ice cream and get right with Jesus

shave my legs just in case

At 6:15, at 8pm, at midnight

when no trump had blown, no fire fallen from the sky, no earthquake or ominous horsemen visited my doorstep

I wiped my hand across my forehead in mock relief and announced

"Whew, dodged that bullet, huh?"

All that fuss and preparation was something to laugh at

how could I take that level of foolishness seriously?

Besides my hair wasn't right

I knew the Lord would not dare let me meet my mother anywhere

near the Rock of Ages

looking like that

I was home-free and safe

But after all the fuss died down

I started to think about how it would really be

I've had Death on my heart lately

He walks a little heavier now than he did before

his footsteps are louder in the empty places created by my

uncertainties

but I still can't believe in millions of hearts ravaged by fear

screaming penance and painful confession

I can't believe in a sudden nothingness

still and barren where the only wine is blood and salt-tears

50 years of AME gospel and Southern Baptist

I'm a white-glove wearing-dyed-in-the-blood-of-the–Lamb-Sunday-
school-teacher-choir girl

I still believe in the rush of angel's wings

lifting me up to stand on line in front of those pearl-white gates and

explain to

Saint Peter

how I did my sinning

believe in Gabriel blowing the opening bars of "Jamaica Funk" and
the stars

falling in Duke Ellington rhythms to light my way home

I believe in every single lyric line of "Swing Low, Sweet Chariot"

because I have been presented with no reasonable alternative

I'm not naïve

I know the devil comes in a thousand faces

breathing horror and destruction in one stinking breath of sulfur

and pain

I know evil tags at the heels of vigilance

waiting for a slip and fall so it can create, then dine

on carrion flesh

and I am as sure of the rush of angels' wings

as I am of the foot-span width of the bridge that crosses over River
Jordan

because I heard Mahaliah's notes

lay certainty in fire

because I heard the Blind Boys of Alabama

set faith in gold and lightning

Because I recognize "Precious Lord, Take My Hand"

is a battle song, not a lullaby

And I know you're saying you want a sign,

not a sermon

a song or symbol

something

to hold your heart together while you figure it out

Then listen

Listen for the wheel and fall of a thousand thousand minutes into an

infinite mystery

watch the sky for raindrops to hump shoulders and shake

like a Harlem ballerina

listen to Mahaliah drop notes that burn

in lightning and fire

This world is not miracles suffocating in an airtight bag

not an arrogant hand waiting to wipe dreams clean and traceless

it's the show, it's the

eloquence of love and incredible pain

the anger created by whimsy and disappointment

it's knowing stars fall down in syncopated Ellington rhythms

It's hearing the difference between a battle song and a lullaby

and understanding how to count a thousand thousand heartbeats

In having the courage to trust your soul

in having the courage to cool your uncertainties

in the lilt and rush

of angels' wings.

32

SEER (FOR AMBER COTE)

She never said it wasn't dangerous

"Child, this is true magic

No word-spinning wisdom

and half-notes of music

will save you here

You got to know!"

I ran anyway

never did have the good sense

not to face down a thunderstorm

·   ·   ·

The fall

down from my fancy

hurt more than love

ever did

without even the consolation

of a pretty sigh

to heal my aches and pains

She looked me up and down

shook her head

She never said it wasn't painful

"Girl, this ain't dust drying up old dreams

you got to pay mind

Understand me, girl?

Stars explode into broken glass

shards rainin' like thunder

if you don't do right!"

       .   .   .

I saw anyway

brought my prophet's eye to the window

and forgot to blink in between

the lies that people tell to themselves

and truth too fragile to be flawless

The resulting blindness

drew tears

like breath suspended in ashes

with no memory of copper-burnt flames

to warm my cheek

She smacked my hand

impatient

clacked her store-teeth

She never said it wasn't hard

"Damn it, this ain't somebody's dream

that can't be captured and made to

sit straight

                    .   .   .

Do you hear me, Girl?

Wind and water embrace, then disappear

women scorn the smell of mist on roses

visions refuse collection

Do you understand?

This ain't slick and easy as passion

Do your job!"

I listened at last

drew fire through my wings

sang half rainbows over full moons

walked back over prism

silver with warning and pride

Finally held my body whole

saw clear through the kiss

of my heartbeat

Blues and Bible stories and conquests

a woman beside the sun

with shadows azure and telling

at her beck and call

smilin' pretty

"You hear me, Child?"

"Yes, Ma'am."

She sighed

and laid her down in sleep

She never said

I'd never get it right.

AFTERWORD

Follow me on this:

I am a Black woman poet; the declaration/clarification is necessary. I want there to be no mistake on how I view/address the way I live my life.

In the last decade, the song of who I am, how this Black woman held it down and held on, became a battle-cry instead of a lullaby. Those years chased/ birthed/ celebrated changes in my voice, and views, that I wasn't always ready for. Yes, a lot of it hurt. A lot. Some of it was downright scary. But I knew this was a true journey, so I bound my wounds and kept moving. (And in the words of my poem FLOW, "looked damn good while I was doing it". Just sayin').

FOLLOW ME ON THIS is truth/homage delivering necessary information. I held on, held it down, and watched the world change in ways I hadn't expected. Fell in and out of love a few times, the way you do. Discovered some things about myself I wish I'd known earlier. Moved (body and soul) about a million times. Let me just say it...my 50's sucked. But that's okay. I'm a Dyson girl; we always land on our feet. This book sings the steps I took afterward.

Right now, every woman in the world stands in the crosshairs of a major upheaval in the way things have always been. No, not the crossroads—we've always been there. Each and every one of us. Because, regardless of country or condition, we have to fight. Or die. We have to sing our songs, because nobody is going to do it for us. Document our days/ dreams/ dares/ desires so the follies that overtake life don't erase us.

Follow me on this. I am a Black woman poet. Singing. LOUD. The definition/clarification is necessary. These poems got me here. Got me home. Built me, branded me, broke me up and down. Poems that celebrate/document/declare my life for this decade, in this world. That way has not been easy. But it is still joyous, and will forever carry the sanity of truth.

ABOUT THE AUTHOR

Stacy Dyson is a poet, acapella vocalist, playwright who specializes in the life and times of the Black woman.

> Someone has to sing for my sisters. Their lives, loves, philosophy...There are centuries of stories begging to be told. I'm lucky enough to be one able to make those voices be heard.

Ms Dyson has done program design, residencies, workshops, and live performances in Colorado, Oklahoma, Massachusetts, New Mexico, South Dakota, Nebraska, Nevada, and all over San Diego.

> But the stage is my natural habitat. It's fine to tell your stories, but for me, unless I can vibe, interact with a crowd, my job is only half-done.

Author of seven collections of poetry (see Also By) are poems, stories and music that "celebrate/document/declare what it is for me to be a Black woman in this world, what it is to be an artist, how myself and my sisters navigate our lives. No, that way is not easy. But it is often joyous, and always carries the sanity of truth."

A former Poet Laureate for Imagination Celebration (Colorado Springs) a nominee for Poet Laureate for the State of Colorado. Founder/ Lead Poet Dragons Wing (Colorado Springs) and CoFounder/ Lead Poet for Page to Stage: Women's Words (San Diego) she is also a Pikes Peak Community Foundation Individual Merit Award recipient, a Colorado Women's Playwriting Festival winner for her play FANNIE'S GIRLS: A 4-1-1 IN-5 PART ATTITUDE, and a TEDx speaker.

 It's never, ever about my single voice. So, the shows and women's workshops are extremely important to me. Especially now, our lives literally depend on knowing how to speak our truth, share our stories, bring thunder and healing with our voices. The workshops are women only because women will say and bring forth deeper parts of their souls when they're surrounded and supported by other women. I've heard stories, confessions… Those conversations, those places have to be given due honor. They have to continue.

Currently, Stacy is promoting her newest collections of poetry LOVELY AND SUFFERING and FOLLOW ME ON THIS. Coming soon is AUGUST 5000, a play about sisters and their relationship, plus a new women's writing/ performance workshop called FIRESCRIBE.

For further information on Stacy Dyson, her voice and vision:

www.saintwinterraines.com

www.wickedhotwords.com

ALSO BY STACY DYSON

~

Author of eight collections of poetry:

- BLACK DIAMONDS
- OBSIDIAN ICE
- BLUES IN THE FIRST POSITION
- WOMAN 724365
- NEFERTIRI'S KISS
- POR INNOCENCIO
- LOVELY and SUFFERING
- and her latest, FOLLOW ME ON THIS

She has also created five CDs of poetry and spoken word.

- THE MADONNA OF NEVADA AVENUE
- POR INNOCENCIO
- A WOMAN BESIDE THE SUN
- SO MANY ANGELS
- and (Love Me) SAN DIEGO STYLE

Her poems, stories and music "celebrate/document/declare what it is for me to be a Black woman in this world, what it is to be an artist, how myself and my sisters navigate our lives. No, that way is not easy. But it is often joyous, and always carries the sanity of truth."

ABOUT RED THREAD PUBLISHING

Stories Change Lives

We believe in the power of women's voices & stories to change the world. We support women not only to write & publish their books but to really embrace their voice, accelerate empowerment & reach global impact. Because women matter.

Do you have a story that must be told?
Sierra Melcher, author & founder of Red Thread Publishing, & our team will support you every step of the way.

www.redthreadbooks.com
info@redthreadbooks.com